Instagram Secrets:

How to Multiply Your Followers and Earn From It

Table of Contents

Introduction

Chapter 1: Building Your Instagram

Chapter 2: Reaching Your Audience

Chapter 3: Optimizing Your Posts

Chapter 4: Using Instagram Features

Conclusion

Description

© Copyright 2018 by Steve Gary - All rights reserved.

The following book is reproduced below with the goal of providing information that is as accurate and reliable as possible. Regardless, purchasing this book can be seen as consent to the fact that both the publisher and the author of this book are in no way experts on the topics discussed within and that any recommendations or suggestions that are made herein are for entertainment purposes only. Professionals should be consulted as needed prior to undertaking any of the action endorsed herein.

This declaration is deemed fair and valid by both the American Bar Association and the Committee of Publishers Association and is legally binding throughout the United States.

Furthermore, the transmission, duplication or reproduction of any of the following work including specific information will be considered an illegal act irrespective of if it is done electronically or in print. This extends to creating a secondary or tertiary copy of the work or a recorded copy and is only allowed with an expressed written consent from the Publisher. All additional rights reserved.

The information in the following pages is broadly considered to be a truthful and accurate account of facts, and as such any inattention, use or misuse of the information in question by the reader will render any resulting actions solely under their purview. There are no scenarios in which the publisher or the original author of this work can be in any fashion deemed liable for any hardship or damages that may befall them after undertaking information described herein.

Additionally, the information in the following pages is intended only for informational purposes and should thus be thought of as universal. As befitting its nature, it is presented without assurance regarding its prolonged validity or interim quality. Trademarks that are mentioned are done without written consent and can in no way be considered an endorsement from the trademark holder.

Introduction

Congratulations on downloading your copy of *Instagram Secrets: How to Multiply Your Followers and Earn From It*. I look forward to helping you build your career as a social media influencer through this book!

We live in an era of social media domination, and the rise of social networking has led to the creation of a whole new breed of career: the social media influencer. Influencer marketing is rising fast as companies realize that platforms like Instagram are booming with untapped potential for reaching all sorts of demographics. Big businesses already got in on the ground floor of this strategy. However, small and medium-sized businesses are looking for new influencers all the time, and that's where your opportunity comes in. With over one billion members joining Instagram since its creation in 2010 and over 500 million active users every day, Instagram is the place to advertise. With this handy guide, you can build a business helping companies to do just that.

This book is the ultimate resource for growing your social media presence, gaining a following, and building a business out of your Instagram! These chapters will teach you how to set up an attractive and professional profile including choosing the best username, profile picture, and bio. You'll also learn what to post, when to post, where to post, and who to post with, as well as insights into creating a feed that is cohesive and pleasing to your audience. Understand how to take full advantage of the many features Instagram offers and build out your brand across the platform. Finally, learn how to begin working with brands when you have as few as 1,000 followers and how to turn your small influence into a big career.

No need to fool you: you won't get rich in a couple of months, but this book will prove itself as a good ally in starting your journey and helping you out in the beginning. It's simple, still complete and useful. Keep it close to you and get started.

There are plenty of books on this subject on the market, thanks again for choosing this one! Every effort was made to ensure it is full of as much useful information as possible, please enjoy!

Chapter 1: Building Your Instagram

    Instagram first came out in 2010. Since then, it has grown to become one of the most popular social networking sites all around the globe. With over 1 billion total users and counting, over 500 million active users are posting, liking, and commenting every day, and this has lead to the rise of a new type of career: the social media influencer. Influencers are individuals with usually large followings who get paid by companies and brands to market their products. Some influencers get loads of free products, free travel, or payments of up to hundreds of thousands of dollars in exchange for posting these brands on an Instagram page for their followers to see. For many people, this career sounds like a dream come true. However, growing a social media following large enough to be an influencer can seem a little daunting, and many people don't know where to start. There is actually a fairly simple strategy to help grow the following you want and turn your Instagram into a brand and a business.

The first step to building a successful Instagram business is building your actual profile. This seems like a simple task, but your username, profile picture, and bio will be very important to the growth of your Instagram presence. The first one is your username. No two Instagram users can have the same username. However, with over 500 million regular users, it can be a little difficult to find the username you want. A catchy pseudonym or phrase based around the type of content your Instagram will contain is the ideal. You want to choose a username that you can build a brand out of. Try to avoid Instagram generated usernames that have a series of numbers or incredibly long run on sentence usernames. A username like "@xyzpurplemountainmonkeyflowerbananatree" will be less likely to gain a following, as will something like "@2154842516515yourname7754763."

If you're creating a travel Instagram, try to incorporate some words associated with travel. As travel Instagrams are quite popular, it may be difficult to find a username with the first few words that come to mind.

Still, if you get a little bit creative, you can create a name that will catch the eye of your followers and be a great addition to your brand. The same goes for fashion, lifestyle, food, etc. Whatever type of content you want to share, choose a name that reflects that. You can also use your actual name. However, this is not usually ideal unless your name is unique and catchy or you already have a following associated with it. If you already have a blog or other social media account, try to keep your Instagram name consistent with those. The idea is to create a brand that your followers will associate with you. The larger presence you have under this brand, the more recognizable and influential it becomes.

Once you have a suitable username, you'll need a profile picture to go with it. Use a square photo that is 500x500 pixels. Choose something that reflects your brand and catches the eye. Instagram currently doesn't allow users to enlarge a profile picture by clicking on it, so it's important to make sure you choose a picture that looks good as a small circle. If you have a logo associated with your brand, you can use it as your profile picture. Otherwise, it's best to use a photo of yourself that is clear and shows your face centered in the frame. If you have a blog or other social media, use the same profile picture for all of them. In the same way, that consistency with your usernames will help create a brand that your followers associate with you. Consistency in profile pictures will put a face to that name as well. If your face is not part of your brand, use your logo or a professional quality photo that reflects your type of content. Just remember that profile photos that have a person in them will relate the best. It also needs to look good in a small frame.

After you've put a name and a face to your brand, it's now time to tell the world what you're all about. You want your bio to relate to your followers and encourage them to want to see more of what you have to share. There are only 160 characters allowed. That is why it's important to make the most of them. Try to avoid using quotes or song lyrics in your bio. This doesn't inspire a look of professionality. Remember that what we're doing here is trying to build a brand and a business. If your Instagram username is not your actual name, it may be good to put your name in the first line of your bio. While a travel Instagram named "@wanderlustexample" might gain followers who like to travel, having a personal touch of the name behind the account can help followers relate more and engage better with your content.

Your bio should describe yourself or your brand in the way that you want to be seen. Still, you have to keep your bio short, sweet, and not self-aggrandizing. If you're running a fashion Instagram, start with something that references your style. "Street style" or "high-fashion cosmopolite" lets people know a little bit of what you represent. It is also helpful to put what country or city you are located in. Not only will this allow people from the same area to relate to your Instagram, but people from other places may also find this interesting.

If you are promoting your skills as a photographer, videographer, makeup artist, or any other artist, this can also allow people who may be near you to reach out and purchase your services. Using Instagram to promote these skills and build your business is very effective. If you have a website or blog associated with your business, insert a call to action in your bio. A call to action is a phrase that encourages your followers to engage with your content. If your blog website or YouTube video is linked to your Instagram, an arrow pointing down toward the link along with a phrase like "Check out my latest blog post!" or "How I style Crocs" will encourage traffic to your posts off Instagram. It also shows your followers that you have valuable content to share with them.

This is the basic content for a professional Instagram bio. There are a couple of formatting tips that can help you present this information in an attractive way. Instagram does not currently allow the addition of line breaks within the app. This can make your bio look like one little run-on sentence, and it won't inspire potential followers to want to read it. If you type out your bio in the Notepad application on your phone, you can insert line breaks, so the information looks crisp and clean.

You can also add emojis, but remember not to go overboard. Instagram is primarily a visual platform, so emojis add a pictorial element to the words in your description. If you travel, add an airplane or globe next to that information in your bio. If your bio includes your base location, you can put the pin drop emoji next to it or the flag associated with your country. Choose emojis that convey your desired image, but make sure they are there to compliment the words you've written, not to be cheesy.

It's also important to remember that if you have a product or service to provide, like photography or fashion styling, your Instagram can be a valuable marketing tool. However, your bio is primarily there to draw people to your Instagram. Let your content be the marketing for your services. Don't try to sell them in your bio.

Be sure to link your website or other social media to your Instagram. If you have a blog or a YouTube channel, putting the URL associated with it in the "Link Website" section of your profile editing tab will make a clickable link that can take your followers directly to your site. If you want to be a social media influencer, creating traffic to your social media is crucial. Linking your Twitter in your Instagram bio and your Instagram in your Twitter bio can allow followers from one form of media to the other. It can also show your followers that you have valuable content to share with them in more than just pictures. If you have a blog, guest writing on other blogs in the same niche can drive traffic to your blog and your social media.

There is also a new feature on Instagram that allows you to add clickable username links or hashtags to your bio. These hashtags do not make your profile visible when the tag is searched, so this isn't really a good way to increase exposure. However, if you collaborate with other Instagrammers, you can tag their profile in your bio in exchange for a tag in their bio. Doing this with Instagrammers from the same niche can raise your exposure to users in your target demographic.

Your username, profile picture, and bio are all part of creating a brand that is associated with you as an influencer. Whatever way you brand yourself, you'll want this to be consistent and an image you can keep up. Looking for big influencers in your niche can be a great way to find inspiration for the brand you want to build. Even so, it should still have your personal spin on it. If you are a photography page, what type of photography are you primarily portraying? You want to build an image that is constantly the same, so your followers can come to rely on and trust who you are. This will build a long-term relationship where your followers appreciate your content.

Followers who trust and rely on what you will post will engage more with your posts and find more value in your social media. Sharing your professional quality photos as a photographer can be a great way to grow your following, but people want to follow pages that have something uniquely valuable to offer. Whether it's natural landscapes, edgy cityscapes, high-fashion portraits, weddings, and families, or whatever your specialty is, a more specific brand of content will let your followers know what to expect from you. This same concept translates no matter what type of Instagram you are growing. Pick a specific type of fashion or a certain aspect of traveling that you regularly portray. You can mix niches like doing fashion and travel together, but you want to make sure that your brand is clear and reliable.

The most profitable niches for Instagram influencers are health and fitness, beauty, travel, business, and fashion. A health and fitness account can be based in various aspects of health or fitness. You can post workout routines to get massive gains or progress pictures to inspire the masses. Maybe your approach to health focuses more on the kitchen and less on the gym, so you must create an account around healthy eating. Whatever spin you take on it, there's a huge following for health and fitness which means a huge potential for success. This also means there's a huge potential for competition. Finding a unique approach to the same concept can prove to be just what many people in your potential audience are looking for in an influencer.

Next is beauty. As with health and fitness, this niche is well saturated with influencers. If you are a makeup artist, hairstylist, or beauty enthusiast, this niche has a lot of potential. This is one of the most well-known areas in which big-name influencers make big bucks. Don't lose hope though. There is still plenty of potential for smaller influencers to get in on the action. Whether you like to create glamorous makeup looks, quick everyday hairdos, or special effects looks, there is an audience for you. If you are also a makeup artist or a hairstylist who provides these services as a part of their business, building an Instagram in this niche can grow your client base exponentially.

The next popular niche for influencers is travel. In 2017, "how to become a travel blogger" was one of the highest searched terms on the internet. Everyone wants to get paid to fill their passport with stamps and their Instagram with blue seas, but it can be hard to get into this world. Becoming a travel blogger may take an investment of your own money in the beginning. Once you've built a feed that inspires the desire to travel, you can start getting brand deals and partnerships that pay you to travel. The traveling niche is filled with smaller niches which are really where you'll find a chance to make a name for yourself. Adventure travel and luxury travel usually reach different audiences. There's travel for retired people, travel for college students, and travel for families with kids. There are also kinds of travel for solo or group, long trips or short trips, etc. Travel is one niche where putting a creative spin on your approach will have a ton of potential to grow you a following.

Business is also a popular niche. Those who have already built business success can share their knowledge via social media and continue growing their careers while helping others. Internet users are always searching for ways to improve their financial success. So, if you know how to help them do so, you can build a brand around helping businesses grow.

The fifth most popular and profitable Instagram niche is fashion. Fashionistas around the world have taken to the Instagram to build their followings and make their fashion dreams come true. This is a great niche to become an influencer in because there are no rules in fashion. Appreciators of fashion love to see new and creative takes, so there is always room to become the next big name in fashion influencing. Smaller niches in the fashion community can include anything from sustainable and eco-friendly fashion for the masses to high fashion creations DIY'd from cheap vintage finds. There's something for everyone, and your personal flair can be just what this community needs.

These 5 major niches are the most profitable on social media these days. However, there are many other options to choose from. Even within these 5 niches, there are hundreds of sub-niches filled with micro-influencers who are building successful businesses.

You want to make sure you choose a brand that is profitable, but you also don't want to brand yourself as something you are not. Remember the fact that genuine presentation of your brand will garner genuine engagement. If who you are is not in line with your brand, it will be difficult to maintain your account. If you create an account based on a traveling lifestyle, but you don't actually do any traveling, you won't have very good content to share with your audience. You want to build an account with unique and genuine content that will provide your audience with a pleasant and valuable experience when they interact with it.

Trying to fake it will not help you make it on the Instagram. Faking followers and likes will also not be beneficial. This is in reference to apps that allow users to purchase followers or likes to increase their "social proof." The idea is that the appearance of having a lot of followers or likes will inspire people to follow them. You can also use apps that give you free likes by liking a stranger's photos. For every 20 likes you give, you can earn 10 likes.

In theory, this may work a little. However, when you start to work with brands or agencies, there are scanners that can be used to check how authentic your engagements and followers are. These websites compare the expected average engagement rates for the following you have with the average engagement rates that you actually achieve. They will also scan through your followers to determine whether the accounts are genuine or bots. This information is then calculated into an authenticity score that reflects whether or not your followers and likes appear to have been purchased. If they have, not only can you be rejected from work with brands or agencies, your Instagram can be banned, and you will have to start over. The best way to become a successful influencer is by building a genuine platform that gains genuine influence.

These concepts are the basis for creating an Instagram that people will want to follow. Make a unique page that offers something your followers can relate to and rely on. Present your brand clearly and be sure that your brand is consistent. Your profile picture and username specifically will become associated with your brand so you won't want to change these if it can be avoided. Your bio can be played with, and different bios can attract different followers. Try different wording, emojis, and formats. Still, always make sure that it is in line with the brand you are trying to project. You don't want to begin representing yourself in a completely different light every week. This will confuse your followers and hinder you from building a genuinely engaged community of followers.

Chapter 2: Reaching Your Audience

Building a great profile is a start, but you can't become an influencer if you don't have an audience to influence. Many people think you need a giant following to be considered an influencer. However, a smaller audience that values your influence and engages with your posts can be just as effective. Many brands are just now realizing the marketing potential of social media. And with price tags of up to $1,000,000 per post, they can't always afford to use top influencers.

A smaller company will look for influencers who have a smaller following but whose followers regularly engage with and value their content. When they want you to represent their product, they are hoping your followers will want to buy it. So, followers who genuinely relate to and value the content of your page will be more likely to give you that credibility.

When you build your brand, you need to figure out what your target audience looks like. If you know who you are catering to, it will be easier to know what to post. For an Instagram dedicated to fashion, you'll clearly want a following of people who also appreciate fashion. But people have all kinds of different styles, so trying to relate to everyone can lead to relating to no one.

To build a genuine following and ensure good engagement, post the type of fashion you relate to most and you will attract like-minded individuals. For instance, if you like street style fashion, post street style consistently. Your goal is to gain influence and be someone that is looked to for inspiration. In the same way that your audience needs to know what to expect from you, you need to know what they want to expect. Engage with your audience and get to know them. Figure out who they are, where they are from, and what they like. Is your audience primarily men or women? What age range are they generally in? Knowing who you're sharing your content with can inspire you to post more relatable content and build a genuine connection with your audience.

There are so many aspiring influencers on Instagram, and many of them are pursuing the same niche audiences because they know that can be profitable. The competition is fierce, but you can be a step above the rest by sharing an aspect of that niche that doesn't get much coverage. One way to ensure you grow a following of people who genuinely appreciate your content is to make content that you would want to see as a follower. For instance, Instagram is chock full of "fitspo" accounts built around inspiring the masses to pursue health and fitness so they can look like these Instagram models. There's a lot of competition to succeed as an influencer in this genre, but there's also a very large and engaged community of people to reach.

If you want to build fitness Instagram, your account will need to incorporate workouts, food, lifestyle choices, inspiration, and such because that is what followers in the fitness community are looking for. However, every other fitness account has those elements too. What element can you bring to the table that maybe they don't? Perhaps you incorporate both fitness and beauty. Share makeup products that won't sweat off, how to preserve the integrity of your hair after swimming in your gym's chlorine pool, or how to style your hair, so it still looks cute after you work out. This is just one example of a way to incorporate a unique twist on a profitable niche to set you apart from the crowd and reach your target audience.

Once your audience is drawn in by your content, you want to keep them around and involved in your page.

Engaging your audience is a great way to help them connect with your content and to build an Instagram presence that people want to follow. The more you respond to comments, the more likely your followers are to comment. Brands who may want to work with you as an influencer will look at your engagement rates to see how invested your followers are in your page. Engagement during the short period directly after you post also affects how much Instagram displays your posts and how relevant your stay is.

Engage with your followers by responding to comments on your posts as well as commenting on their posts. When commenting on other user's photos, avoid using generic comments like "love this" or "good post." Most importantly, don't just put a heart eyes emoji. Try to make sure your comments are as genuine and relevant to the post as possible. It doesn't have to be a paragraph about their photo, but a reference to the caption or the content of the photo shows that you took the time to appreciate their content and that the engagement is genuine. Seeing this makes the recipient more likely to do the same for you.

Chapter 3: Optimizing Your Posts

Posting good content is an important part of being an Instagrammer. However, there's still more to good content than just pretty pictures. In 2016, Instagram replaced the chronological feed with an algorithm that shared more relevant posts first rather than most recent. Users were not fond of this algorithm change, especially aspiring influencers. One of the primary factors that were now taken into account to determine how much exposure your posts got was how much engagement they received in the first 30 minutes or so after posting. This meant that if you posted at a time of day when not many people were active, your followers might not even see your post when they do log on. In 2018, Instagram announced that they will be updating the algorithm again to ensure posts show up more chronologically, but relevance is still an important factor. To ensure that your posts get the maximum exposure, you need to learn and know what, when, and how to post contents effectively.

First, what you're posting is obviously important to your page. This is what your audience follows you for. You want to create regularity in what you post, so your audience has a reliable type of post to associate with you. Some people take this to the extremes. What this really means is that you want to create consistency in the look and feel of the images you post so they will present cohesively when displayed next to each other on your Instagram page. This involves what you're posting pictures of, how you are editing your pictures, the captions you are posting with them, and the value they are giving to your audience.

When you find your niche and create your brand, you want to stick to it. Post pictures that fit into that brand and avoid straying from those pictures. If your Instagram account is dedicated to creative ways to ice cupcakes, you should probably be avoiding posting pictures of your cat and your new shoes unless they are somehow relevant to cupcakes. Your followers expect a certain type of content, and they may be confused by changes in what you're sharing. This can drop engagement rates and even make you lose followers.

You'll also want to keep some kind of consistency in the angles, backgrounds, crop size, and color scheme of your photos. For a fashion Instagram, 2 or 3 cool poses or angles can be used consistently to showcase the outfits you're sharing. This allows your followers to associate your brand with a specific look, even though the styles aren't the same. Cropping your pictures to the same size will also create an association between your posts and a specific presentation. More horizontal crops like a landscape style don't present well on Instagram. However, if this crop fits well with the type of photos you are posting, you can make it work. A 4x5 crop (400 pixels by 500 pixels) makes your photo an optimal size to post on Instagram. This is the largest vertical size allowed. When you post a photo this way, it fills the majority of the screen when your followers scroll past it on their timeline. Making sure your photo is this size before you want to post it will prevent you from having to crop the top or bottom off of it in the Instagram app. You can always choose a different size, but consistency is the key.

Try to also keep some consistency in the background or in the color scheme. You don't have to always be in front of a brick wall or a bright green nature scene. Though, if you run a street style fashion account, you may want to stick to urban settings. Posting videos will also increase engagement. When videos are posted on Instagram, they show the number of views received rather than the number of likes received. This number is usually much higher, and when followers see this, it can make them more inclined to engage with your post. Videos also allow you to be more genuine on your profile and mimic an in-person engagement much better. This method may bring about a more positive response from your audience.

Having a consistent editing style will help you create some cohesivity in your feed. This makes sure that the colors that are present in your photos generally look the same in every photo. Using apps like VSCO allows you to create presets so that you can use to utilize the same filter, temperature setting, contrast, highlights, and such in every photo. This can be very helpful. However, it may be better to stick to editing each photo on an individual basis. This allows you to tweak different small aspects that benefit that specific photo.

You can also use the filters in the Instagram app. Photos with one of a few specific filters tend to get higher engagement than others, so using these may increase the favorability of your posts. Clarendon, Gingham, and Juno are the 3 most popular filters, followed by Lark and Mayfair. Using these filters or similar filters from other apps can increase engagement on your photos.

You can also incorporate a specific personal touch that you can add to each of your photos. Some people like to post photos with an element of darkness or shadows. Doing this consistently can draw an audience and keep them engaged to look forward to seeing how you incorporate this element. It can narrow down the photos you are able to post, but it will also help grow the number of your followers. Having one color that is present in each photo (for instance, a red shirt in one photo, a red building awning in the background of another, and a red coffee mug on a table in yet another photo) can be enough of an element of consistency.

How you caption your photos can also be important. The caption should be relevant to the photo in some way. It should also add to the feel of the photo and not take away from it. Really long captions are a bit iffy in how they can be read by your audience. An unnecessarily long-winded caption can detract your audience from the beauty of your photo. This can cause your followers to not hit the like button because they get distracted by reading the caption and scroll on. A long caption that educates your followers on a topic within your brand can be a positive addition to your posts as it gives your followers something useful. This creates a value exchange. Your followers will be engaged with your posts and therefore, help you grow your Instagram presence because they are receiving something worthwhile from your content.

A short, basic caption may be fine, but it won't catch the eye. Try to avoid the overuse of emojis. However, you can use them to add emotion to what your caption says and lend a more visual element to your words. Song lyrics are usually not a good option for captions especially if you are creating a professional Instagram. They can only be incorporated if they are relevant to your brand, used ironically, or used in part of an insightful caption.

You can also include a call to action (CTA) in your caption. CTAs like "tag a friend who ____" or "like this if you ____" can increase engagement. This is a very important part of a caption and is always included if necessary especially when you want your audience to buy products from you. You can also ask a question of your audience and follow with "leave an answer in the comments." Using a call to action is not quite as effective until you have at least 1,000 followers or a dedicated follower base. Once you do have a reliable following, you can leverage the follower base you already have to gain exposure. You can host competitions where you give your followers an opportunity to receive a good item or service that they would value in exchange for them sharing your post, tagging a friend, or getting a small number of friends to follow your account and say who they were sent by. These tactics are an obvious method to grow your following. Your followers won't mind doing so especially if your content is valuable.

Geotags and hashtags are also a great way to increase the exposure of your posts and up your engagement rates. Every post you make should have a geotag as this can increase your engagement rates by up to 79 percent. This can either be the name of the city or country you are in or the name of the specific location depending on the type of photo you're posting. When Instagram users search for a location, the photos that are tagged there show up as Top Posts or Most Recent posts. Top Posts are generally the photos or videos from this location that have had the largest engagement. If you use a local restaurant name as your location, your chances of being in the Top Posts section when the restaurant is searched are much higher than if you use just the country you are in as your geotag. If you are in a major city, using the city name as the location can create exposure by putting you on the Most Recent section, but this will likely be short-lived because the geotag is used frequently, so the new posts will push yours further and further down the page.

Hashtags pose the same type of issue. Using the most popular hashtags is a great way to gain exposure for your photos because users are frequently looking through these hashtag threads for cool posts. The problem with this is there are already so many photos being posted online with popular hashtags causing the exposure to be over very quickly. You can use up to 30 hashtags on each photo, but it's advised to keep it at a maximum of 15, so it doesn't overwhelm your caption box. You can also add your hashtags in a comment after posting the photo. Remember that this has to be done quickly if you want your photo to show up on the Most Recent page.

To gain maximum exposure, use a few well-trafficked hashtags to increase immediate engagement. You can also use less well-trafficked hashtags that pertain to your brand. The top 5 Instagram hashtags are #love, #instagood, #photooftheday, #tbt, and #beautiful. A quick Google search can yield a list of over 150 popular hashtags. So, if these 5 aren't relevant to your photo, you can use something else. Use a few of these well-frequented but generic tags, but also use tags that will be frequented by your target audience. A fashion account may tag "ootd", "instastyle," or "fashionblogger" to reach the larger fashion community, but you can also add "modestfashion" or "grungechic" to reach an audience looking for a specific style.

Tagging companies, brands, or feature accounts can also increase exposure. If you tag a large brand, they may, in turn, like or comment on your post which can cause it to be shown as a suggested post to their followers. If your photos are of very good quality, some brands or companies may even ask to repost your photo on their page or in their Instagram story. This allows your post to be seen by a much larger group of people and some of that audience may decide to follow you.

Tagging featured accounts may also increase exposure as they will share your photos and your username. Many of the followers on these pages will be willing to follow and engage with your posts.

Consistently posting Instagram stories can also maintain relevance and increase engagement. When you post photos and videos to your story, you allow your followers to be a part of your daily life and also to involve you as part of theirs. Using features like the poll or question features can give incentives for your followers to interact with your story. This may also lead them to respond more to your stories in the future. Opening up this kind of engagement will increase the likelihood of their engagement with the other posts. Posting daily on Instagram stories maintains this presence.

Also, posting frequently throughout the day will ensure that your story is one of the first shown when your followers open Instagram. Stories are shown from left to right with the most recent first leading to the less recent. You can also use a call to action in your story after you post a photo or video to your feed. Take a screenshot of your profile and place an emoji or blur over where the most recent photo is shown. Caption this with a call to action inviting your followers to look at your new post. This has been the traditional way of self-promoting posts.

However, there's a new feature on Instagram that also allows you to share posts directly to your story. It will share the picture with a clickable link to your username or the username of whatever account's photo you share. This can be an effective tool for collaborating with other creators. As soon as they post, share their photo or video to your story with a call to action for your followers to check it out. This can increase engagement in their post in the crucial minutes and hours after posting so that the photo or video gets more exposure from the Instagram's algorithm. When you exchange this type of service with the other creators in a similar niche, you can expose each other's content to an audience that will appreciate it. This benefits both the creator and the audience.

Now, we've covered a lot of the ins and outs on what to post, what photos to use, how to present them on your feed, captioning, hashtagging, brand tagging, and the likes. One of the other key elements of gaining exposure and increasing engagement is WHEN you're posting. This includes what time of day your photos are going up, how frequently you're posting them, and how consistently you're posting them.

The best times of day to post are the times when most users are active. In 2018, this is usually at lunchtime between the hours of 11 o'clock in the morning and 1 o'clock in the afternoon, or when people are relaxing at the end of the day between 7 o'clock and 9 o'clock in the evening. It can also be beneficial to post in the mornings when people check their phones, but they are less likely to engage with posts in the morning than the afternoon or evening. Wednesdays and Thursdays tend to be the days with the highest engagement levels while weekends see a drop in engagement because people are usually not spending quite as much time on their phones.

It's also important to know where in the world your most active followers are located so you can post at optimal times in their specific time zones. If you live in the United States, but the majority of your engagement comes from England, 7 to 9 in the evening for you is not going to be the same for your followers. There are apps available to let you track when your engagement levels are highest as well as having an option to schedule your posts during high engagement hours. If you switch to an Instagram business profile, these demographic breakdowns will be available for free as part of your profile after you reach 10,000 followers. You'll know what regions the majority of your followers are in, what age range they fall into, and what percentage are male or female. So, once you've ensured that your posts are going up at the right times, you want to make sure that you are posting at these times consistently and frequently.

At the very least, you should be posting once a week, but you can generally post up to 3 times a day without being considered overboard. Once a week might maintain a following that you already have, but it won't be likely to help you grow a following. If you haven't been posting regularly, increasing your frequency by 3 or 4 posts a week can help your following grow quickly. After you've increased your Instagram presence, posting as close to once a day is recommended as you can grow your following exponentially. This is because people know that you will provide consistent content. You can increase this amount until you're posting twice a day, but cap it at 3 posts per day. It can also help to post at the same general time(s) every day. This allows your followers to begin expecting your posts, so they'll be more likely to be active during those times and increase their engagement.

Collaborating with other Instagrammers can also increase engagement. Engagement groups or pods are groups of Instagrammers who like or comment on the posts of others in the group in exchange for likes and comments on their own posts. Some of these groups will have scheduled posting windows called rounds. If a group has a scheduled round at 11 o'clock in the morning eastern time, anyone in the group who wants to participate will enter his or her username around 30 minutes before the 11 o'clock start time. The coordinator or bot will then make a list of the usernames and send it to the group. The participating members will post their photos or videos just before 11 and then they'll go through the list of usernames and like or comment on the new post. In some cases, the members will then inform the group when they've completed liking and commenting posts. Some engagement groups don't operate in rounds. Instead, members just drop a link to their post into the group when it is posted, and the other members can like and comment of their own volition.

These groups can be a great way to increase the initial engagement on your post. This tells the Instagram algorithm that your post is relevant and thus, increases the exposure. These engagement groups are also a good way to find Instagrammers to collaborate with. Collaborations can be done by trading shoutouts on stories or simply mentioning or tagging other accounts in a post. Shoutouts can begin to annoy your followers so be careful about this. Sharing a good reason why you like the account and why your followers also will is much more likely to get a positive reaction from your audience than "Shoutout to @_____ GO FOLLOW THEM."

You can also use the Instagram live option to stream with another account. This will reach both your followers and theirs. Live streams are also beneficial because, on your followers' Instagram feed, it will show live streams in the same bar as stories. Live streams can stay on this bar for 24 hours if you choose which increases your followers' interaction with your content.

Sharing quality content is important. To become an influencer, you do need to post content that people want to consume, but this isn't enough. If you want to gain an audience and increase engagement, you need to increase the exposure your photos are receiving. Knowing your audience, posting the right type of photos, and increasing the frequency and timing of your posts will optimize engagement with the audience you already have. Hashtagging and geotagging can also increase engagement with prospective followers. Be sure to continue to engage with your followers by responding to comments, liking and commenting on their posts, and responding to messages, at least occasionally.

Chapter 4: Using Instagram Features

Instagram has introduced a few new features that are making it one of the best social media platforms available. When it comes time to post a photo, and you can't pick between 2 or 3 amazing ones, don't worry. Post all three with the multi-photo feature. Add fun effects to your stories, and if you end up with a really great story, you can feature it on your profile long after its original 24 hours is up. Some regions now have the music feature that allows you to play music in your stories from the Instagram app itself. There are also filters, direct messages, and video calling available to use. The list of Instagram features that you can use goes on. Making the most of Instagram's features will help you take full advantage of what Instagram has to offer and maximize the exposure and engagement of your posts.

One of the features that have been released is the ability to add a clickable hashtag or username to your profile's bio. This can be beneficial if you've created a hashtag for your page. Making your own hashtag that relates specifically to your profile and the content you share can help your audience form a community around your profile which will increase engagement and spread the word. You can add a call to action with the hashtag and inspire your followers to use it. If you have other Instagram accounts, you can also link these in your bio, although, this is less recommended. This feature may be better used in collaborations. An account with a similar target audience may agree to tag you in their bio if you do the same. These are small ways to use this feature as an aid in growing your Instagram.

The "Collections" feature can be helpful when you're looking for inspiration on how to pose, color schemes, or caption ideas. You should never be a copycat, but learning from brands and influencers is perfectly okay. If you're scrolling through your feed and see a photo that you might want to take inspiration from, you don't need to screenshot it. Save your gallery space for Insta-worthy photos. Simply touch the small bookmark icon on the bottom right-hand side of the photo to add it to your collection. Only you can see what you save to your collection, and it can be accessed from your profile next to the icon for tagged photos. You can create different collections for different things, i.e., style inspo, post inspo, photography inspo, recipes to try, etc., and sort the posts as you'd like. This can be a helpful tool for learning from what content already exists to make an even better content.

Instagram stories are an important tool for communicating with your audience and growing your following. As we mentioned before, posting daily to your story allows your followers to become accustomed to seeing you regularly and to feel like they are sharing in your experiences. This builds a genuine connection that can increase engagement rates. It is also a way for you to share content that is slightly outside of your niche posting, but only occasionally. If you run a fashion Instagram, you should stick to fashion in your actual posts. However, posting your dog or a pretty latte you bought onto your story can increase relatability without hindering your brand.

The story features that Instagram has released can be utilized in various ways to optimize engagement. You can post photos, videos, or text posts. Incorporating all of these features can keep your content fresh and enticing for the audience. Post videos and selfies to share important or inspirational information. These don't always have to be entertaining or informative, but you don't want your audience to lose interest. You can also post text-only stories that have one of a few color backgrounds and font options. These can be a great resource for announcements, coupon codes, events, promotions, or giveaways. Try not to overuse the text-only posts as this can lead your audience to swipe away from your story when they get tired of reading. If they swipe past your story frequently, you will start to show up lower and lower on their story list.

The poll option and question option are great ways to interact with your followers. With the poll option, you can ask a question, and your followers can choose an answer from the list of options. After 24 hours, the answers will be tallied in a final percentage, and you can share your results with your audience. The question feature is an even better way to engage your audience because you can respond to their answers. What this feature entails is a sticker in which you write a question or a statement, and when you post it to your story, your followers will have the option to respond in the text box. You will receive all of the responses along with being able to tell who sent in the answer. If you choose, you can repost the responses to your story with commentary. The name of the person where the replies are from will not show in your story unless you add it.

You can also add gifs, stickers, mentions, and locations to the stories. These are fun ways to spice up your photos or videos and to shout out brands or accounts. When you do tag brands or accounts in your story, they can now repost it to their own story, and vice versa. This can be useful when you start working with brands as an influencer because if they like your story, they may share it and increase your exposure. You can also use this feature for shouting out other accounts when you're trying to help each other's audiences grow. You can also share posts to your story. This can be used when shouting out other accounts, or in self-promotion. When you see a post you want to promote, hit the button that you would normally use to send it in a direct message. This will give you the option of sharing the post to your story. When you do this, it will post the photo with a clickable link to the username of the post. This is a great alternative to the "screenshot and post" method of promoting your new photos and can be a helpful tool in promoting friends, brands, and other accounts.

    A related feature that was recently released is the Instagram TV feature. IGTV, as it's more commonly called, is a new long-form video platform that is available in the Instagram app or in its own app. Videos can be up to an hour long and are in the same vertical format as Instastories. Unlike stories, these videos remain on IGTV in the same way your posts remain on your profile. For influencers who don't have a blog or Youtube channel, this can create an opportunity to make video content that promotes brands and products more than a simple photo or story. Videos are full screen and vertical so you can watch them without having to turn your phone. This creates a different feel than YouTube and is a new type of long-form video platform. Taking advantage of the benefits of IGTV is important, especially while it is still new.

A really great feature that is less related to building your Instagram presence and more related to dealing with a growing Instagram presence is the anti-hate features that have recently been added. In your settings, there is now an option under comment controls that allows you to hide offensive comments. This will hide any comment that appears to contain a threat to your health and well-being or an attack on your character or appearance. As your following on social media grows, you may encounter rude comments from irrelevant people. Instagram has taken strides to prevent this type of hate, as well as blocking hashtags that are regularly used for bullying or posting inappropriate content.

Switching your Instagram account to a business profile can give you access to a host of features that will greatly benefit your growth as an influencer. Some features aren't available until you reach 10,000 followers, but it may still be worth it to become a business profile before this point. You'll need to have a Facebook business page to connect to your Instagram, and you'll need to make sure you have admin access to this page. Then, you'll choose a category to classify your business in. For example, if you're a blogger, you can brand yourself as a personal blog. This will also help people who come across your profile to be aware right away of what your general brand is.

One of the great features of switching to a business account is that you can then add your email address, phone number, or business address, and it will be available on your profile. In the past, influencers and businesses had to try to include this information in their bio, along with the rest of their bio contents. This is the basic setup for a business profile. One of the primary rewards for having a business account is that you'll gain access to Instagram Insights. Many influencers have been paying money to third-party apps to have their profiles analyzed to better understand their audience and how to reach them. With Insights, you can see a breakdown of how your posts perform at different times and on different days, as well as understanding your target demographic better. You can see what percent of your audience is men and what percent are women, as well as the general age range of the majority of your followers and the approximate location of the majority of your most engaged followers. This information can help you better understand when to post, what to post, and whom you're really reaching.

Instagram has also released a lot of new features and an updated algorithm. Now, it's even easier to create great content and reach a larger audience. Making sure that your social media content is permeating every aspect of Instagram's many features will help you build a presence that followers can rely on and appreciate. This will build your influence and lead you to be an asset to brands and businesses as an influencer.

Chapter 5: Finding Brands to Work With

Once you've built your audience, you'll want to start collaborating with brands and businesses. Most people think you need to have a huge following before you can start to promote and collaborate, but you can get started with as little as 1,000 followers. You won't be seeing big money, or probably any money at first, but consistently building your presence and credibility as an influencer will lead to bigger options later on. Having a blog, YouTube channel, or other active social media where you have some kind of following is very helpful. It's not entirely necessary, but the more, the merrier. Brands will likely not approach you when you have a small following. If they do, it might be the sketchier brands that you want to avoid. However, you can start working with brands by approaching them first.

Smaller businesses are usually the first clients for budding influencers. Some brands will try to reach out to people who want to be influencers and offer affiliate discount codes and "exposure" in return for buying their products. These businesses usually don't have high-quality products, and promoting them may not be good for your credibility. The affiliate discount codes they will give you operate by earning you free products based on how many of your followers purchase using your discount code. This can be an enticing idea, but remember that the quality of these products is usually not very great. The "free products" that you will earn are usually the cheapest they offer and are not something you can choose. These businesses may even ask you to purchase a product initially, but they will convince you to do so by offering to repost the photos you take and promoting the product so you will have more exposure. This is an option to start out as an influencer or to gain exposure if you want to risk working with these companies, but it is not advised and really doesn't help your credibility as an influencer.

If businesses do not approach you, you can certainly approach them. Look through hashtags to find small businesses with products that you and your followers will like. You can also do a Google search for a product that you want to promote and try to find small businesses that carry something similar. Look through their products and find what exact product (or products) you would like to promote, and then email the business. Because this is a business transaction, do not communicate through direct messages. If the business doesn't have an email address on their Instagram page, look on the website for a press email or customer service email. Sometimes, this can be hard to find. Another option is to direct message the company and ask for an email address you can use to communicate with them. Once you have their email, contact them via that avenue. Be sure you are using a professional email address, not one of those email accounts you made in 10 years ago like purplerainbowunicorns9823798@example.com. This type of email address does not reflect well on business transactions. Once you've established a name for your brand or yourself, consider creating an email address that is specifically for business transactions as an influencer. When you're ready to email the company, be sure you know what to say. It can be helpful to keep a template in a document and alter it to meet the needs of each communication.

Your email should read something like this:

Hello, my name is (Your Name).

I am an influencer based in (example city), and I post about (fashion, health, travel, etc.). I also do (photography, videography, run a blog, etc.) that can be viewed on my website www.examplewebsite.com.

I'm interested in working with your company and featuring your products on my Instagram @exampleInstagramhandle/Twitter/Youtube/Blog. Here are a few examples of how I'd like to feature your products:

(Insert at least three examples of previous product promotions OR posts where a product is prominent and noticeable. If you don't have these, link posts that are of good quality and have a higher number of likes and comments.)

Your products would be a great fit for my audience. Altogether, my audience consists of ___ individuals over various social media platforms, and I'd like to share your products with them to introduce them to your brand. The majority of my audience are (men, women, mothers, travelers, etc.) who would appreciate and use your products, and I'd specifically like to share (specific product) in (idea for the post type, setting, number of posts, etc.).

I look forward to working with you,

(Your Name)

This is a basic email template, but it gives you an idea of how to approach a brand. Each section should be between 3 and 5 sentences long, but try not to exceed 5 sentences. Stating where you are based can be especially useful if you are reaching out to local companies. If you have a website, you can include it to show that you have more to offer than just Instagram posts. If you only have Instagram, that is fine also. Make sure to send the name of your Instagram profile so they can see the quality of your content and what your feed looks like.

If you have past experience with promoting brands, include the photo and a link to the post. If you don't have this experience, include links to posts where products are prominently featured, even if they are not sponsored. This is one reason it can be beneficial to tag companies whose products are prominent in your pictures. In the case that you don't have any of these posts, include posts that show quality content or create an idea of the setting in which you'd like to feature the product. Try to use posts with a higher engagement.

Next, explain why this specific company is a good fit for your brand and why your audience will want to purchase their products. This not only tells them why they're a good fit for your platform, it also shows that your platform can be a good fit for them. Finish the email with a proposal on how you can feature their product. Because you are approaching the brand first and not the other way around, it's best to come in with an idea. Social media marketing directors and press agents are busy people. They may greatly appreciate not having to create a concept for how their product can be featured, and it may save them a lot of time if they were searching for an influencer.

If they choose not to work with you, don't get discouraged. There are plenty of other companies out there. Instagram marketing is a growing field, and new companies are entering the world of online influencing daily. If they do want to work with you, be sure to clarify how many posts you are agreeing to do in exchange for the product. When you're just starting out, you probably won't receive money for posts. If they do offer, base your asking price on the size of your following and your engagement. 66 percent of companies won't pay over $250 for an Instagram post, and most won't pay at all unless you're at least a mid-sized influencer (30,000 followers and up). Since you're approaching the businesses in this situation, you can't really ask for money. Exchanging one post and a couple of Instastories for a product is usually fair for products that are less than $100. For products that are a little more expensive, one post, a couple of Instastories, and a blog post might be more suitable. Be sure to clarify with the company what they expect out of the exchange.

When you receive the product, email the company and let them know that you got it. You should promote the product as soon as possible. If you won't be able to post right away, be sure to inform the company and give them an idea of when exactly you will be able to post it. Once the post is up, send them the actual photo that you posted as well as a link to the post. In this way, they don't need to screenshot the photo to get a copy of it, and they don't need to search for your Instagram to see the post. This kind of courtesy may also lead the same company to be willing to work with you in the future. If you enjoyed their product and the exchange went well, thank them and ask if they'd be open to working together again in the future.

One important part of being an influencer is only promoting brands you actually like. At the beginning of their influencer careers, many people will try to promote any company that will work with them. If a product doesn't fit your brand, isn't marketable to your audience, or is simply not a good product, promoting it can do more harm than good to your credibility. You want to make good quality content to promote products, and that involves a lot of time and effort. Do not waste your hard work on working with companies you don't genuinely want to promote to your followers. Posts you are passionate about will also usually end up being higher quality because you care about them more.

Once brands start to approach you, be on the lookout for red flags. If a company approaches you offering a product promotion in exchange for exposure, be wary. A company approaching you is asking to work with you. You should send your asking rate and proceed with the deal from there. Some companies will offer that you can get exposure and a part in an affiliate program instead of payment. An affiliate program is when you are given an affiliate link to share with your followers, and in turn, you get a minuscule portion of the profits from each purchase made through your link. This is not worth much in the grand scheme as it requires that your followers go through your specific link. So, if they just go to the company's website you get nothing. Sometimes, companies do this instead of paying up front because it costs them less in the long run.

Another way they try to avoid paying is by offering the first product promotion as a "trial run" with potential for a paying business relationship later on. Generally, these businesses will not end up following through on this long-term relationship. It's just a tactic to avoid paying for marketing. Companies may also agree to pay you but try to offer you significantly less than your asking price. Especially once you are established as an influencer, if you tell your rates to a company, and they offer you a significantly less amount, it may be a red flag. They may simply not have the budget, and you can still choose to work with them if it's a company you really want to promote. However, if they also diminish the value of your time and effort in promoting their product or act like they are doing you a favor by working with you, do not work with that company.

Some businesses that don't have the budget to pay influencers may still offer products in exchange. If a business offers you products in exchange for promotion but doesn't let you choose the products, this is an indicator that they may not be a good fit for you as an influencer. You want to work with companies that value you as a good fit for their brand, and you want to value them as a good fit for your audience. Not being involved in product selection is one small way that businesses show that it may not turn out to be the best working relationship.

Once you start gaining a following, you can join an influencer agency. Some agencies will work with you when you have as little as 2,000 followers, but others will require a larger audience. Working with an agency is a great way to make sure you receive fair compensation for the work you exerted into putting out quality content. Agencies will negotiate with companies on your behalf and help you find businesses that suit your brand. This can help you in maintaining a consistent brand and only promoting products that will be a good fit for your audience.

You can start working with brands even when you have a small audience. When you do work with brands, be sure that's not all you are posting about. As an influencer, you are primarily creating content for your audience, not for brands. If your feed starts to look like a constant ad campaign, you may lose the relatability and genuineness you had built with your audience. The biggest benefit of being a smaller influencer is that you are relatable to your followers and have higher engagement rates than a big name influencer. Take advantage of that fact. Promote products you genuinely support and want to share with your followers, and don't do it just for the money.

Conclusion

Thank you for making it through to the end of *Instagram Secrets: How to Multiply Your Followers and Earn From It*. I hope it was informative and able to provide you with the right advices to start building your social media empire into a prosperous business.

Now, you know how to create a profile that will grab and hold the attention of your target audience. You've also learned how to find your brand and build a following, and you've got all the tools to make your content beautiful, consistent, and unique. You can now start increasing your social media presence, upping your engagement rates, and building your brand into a booming business. Once you have a couple thousand followers, you can start reaching out to businesses using the helpful tips in this book and get a portfolio of product promotions under your belt to help you in future business partnerships. This book is a compilation of the tips and tricks that very successful influencers used to grow their brand into a business, and they can do the same for you!

Remember! Don't ever focus your attention only on the number of followers, instead consider the people as an interested audience, which cares about your content and actively interacts with you. Most of the time, smaller Instagram accounts are more profitable than the biggest ones, due to the fact that they can rely on a targeted audience with higher engaging rates. Quality – rather than quantity – matters the most.

I suggest you again to start looking for small businesses that needs their products promoted: they're easier to reach, allow you to start gradually and don't need huge numbers use your services. This is your starting point. Big companies will come to you later, as soon as you grow a booming audience.

Finally, I want to personally thank you for reading this book; if you found it useful in any way, a review on Amazon is always appreciated!

SIC PARVIS MAGNA, greatness from small beginnings.

www.ingramcontent.com/pod-product-compliance
Lightning Source LLC
Chambersburg PA
CBHW070957240526
45469CB00016B/1529